Show Up Empty

A Guide To Identifying and Activating Your Gifts

Tawanda La'Shan Story

Copyright © 2016 Tawanda La'Shan Story
All rights reserved.

ISBN: 1523867558
ISBN 13: 9781523867554

This book is dedicated to my father Wayne Story Sr. for being with me every step of the way and to my daughter, Paris Olivia Cooper for inspiring me to keep going even when you didn't know you could.

Table of Contents

When I Say Empty, I Mean Empty

You Have The Greatness Gene

Uncomfortable Enough To Move

~Gift Check~

Trash Day

Bread Crumbs

~Gift Check~

Assembly Required

~The Promises~

You Be The Expert

Invest In You

Using The Erasable Ink Pen

Hustling VS. Gifting

Palpitations & Purpose

~ Gift Check~

Seek God For Clarity-He's The Master Builder

Fail Until You Fly

Let Them See Your Scars

Serve As If Your Life Depends On It

How Will I Know I'm Empty?

Forward

We choose educational paths and careers based on our strengths in that area or because it is something we enjoy doing. Perhaps, it is simply because we are good at it. We become so engulfed in these choices, that we negate the fact that although this particular chosen avenue has been somewhat successful and perhaps even financially fruitful, it is not the only gift or talent strategically embedded within us by the Creator himself. Each of us have been very uniquely created and designed with multiple gifts and talents, and each of these were placed inside of us to ignite sparks and fires for our next level of experiences. Whether it is fear of failure or fear of actually being successful, we somehow suppress those unused gifts and talents when they were actually intended to elevate and propel us into greatness and success! Oftentimes, it seems easier to sit and watch others become successful, live fruitful lives, and display their many gifts than to put in the work to activate and release your own gifts.

Show Up Empty is a guide to help you identify all of your gifts and talents and instructions on what to do with them once identified. Your time spent here on earth should be filled with experiences, failures, opportunities and risks. That's the beauty of recognizing your gifts.

I must caution you though that after reading this guide, you may experience a strong sense of entrepreneurship and creative independence. These are some of the emotions that come along with being obedient to God's will in your life and activating your gifts.

God has equipped each of us with an abundance of gifts and talents and there is no customer service desk in Heaven to make return transactions. Therefore, we must fervently seek opportunities to use every talent and gift that we have. Prepare to be amazed at what is living inside of you and just waiting to be groomed, nurtured and developed. After all, He promised us a full and rich life!

So, Show Up Empty where you ask? In Heaven of course. Do not return to your maker and creator with unused gifts and talents. It is my belief that He wants to welcome us all emptied out of the very specific and unique gifts and talents designed just for us only to fill is up again but this time with the ultimate gifts. Let's get started on maximizing your potential.

When I Say Empty, I Mean Empty!

While writing Show Up Empty, I believe that God strategically placed a roller coaster in the middle of my life. Many thought that I was striving to be Superwoman, when really I was doing all that I could to keep my head up.

The vision for Show Up Empty came the same year my father suffered the first of three debilitating strokes. That alone was enough to make even me surrender. There wasn't enough nurse, daughter, or health care professional in me to help me handle and process this.

After the first stroke and fall that resulted in a brain injury, I decided to move my father in with me and become his primary caregiver. Meanwhile I was running my Home Health Care business and nonprofit agency. My daughter was in her second year of college at Jackson State University, I was the Youth Choir Director at my church, designed jewelry and bow ties by hand, and the promise I made to my community to take care of our seniors kept my phone ringing at all times for resources and support. Every day someone who loved me but couldn't relate to my purpose, my passion, or my calling would offer their advice and say, "You need to let some things go." While I appreciated the concern that was genuine, I couldn't let my candle go out. Something on the inside of me was burning my wick mighty low but ignited my fuel at the same time. **(Highlight This! I know you can relate)**

I remember thinking to myself, "God, you've got to be kidding me! In the midst of all of these trials, I'm supposed to focus and write a book?" It seemed like every day brought about a new trial, a new struggle, and a new hurt. I didn't know at times if I was coming or going but I did realize that all of these things placed before me were essential for my growth, essential for my faith, and essential for my ME!

I kept waiting for a place of release, a place of rest but I eventually saw the meaning of it all. As much as I wanted to give up and quit, I couldn't. Although I felt as though I had earned the right to quit, I couldn't! None of it was easy, but somehow I had just enough energy and strength to keep pushing. God knew that all of these things were going to happen and he equipped me for them and I had no idea.

(Highlight This!) If you focus and pour out all that you have into our endeavors, I promise you He will meet you in the middle and supply every need, open every door, and orchestrate every divine connection. There will be times that you don't want to Show Up Empty because you simply don't feel like it. You may feel as if you have nothing else to give, but He who created you knows your limitations and just how much is in you.

He will continue to strengthen you to identify and use every gift that you have. None of your trials will ever be larger than God so why allow them to stop you from reaching your next level?

Do You Know What Gifts You Have?

1. _____

2. _____

3. _____

4. _____

5. _____

So you can't think of five gifts? No worries! We will revisit this later.

Once you have recognized your gifts and talents, remember that taking them all to Heaven is not an option. They have no trade in value. Be willing to share with others how you became successful.

#showupempty

You Have The Greatness Gene

One of the things that drove me so passionately to write my first book about utilizing gifts, was hearing people say to me "I wish I had your drive" or "I wish I had your energy". I grew tired of saying, "But you do!" Your gift may not be my gift but you have your own and once you realize what THEY are, you too can begin to walk in their manifestation.

My experience of course, is centered on my heritage and my culture. I didn't have to do much research or interview anyone to know that I come from a culture of people created with a certain mixture of tenacity, strength, and the ability to be great! There is no denying that it is in our DNA, it is who we are and how we are designed. We often see greats like Michael Jordan and Oprah Winfrey in the spotlight, and seem to somehow forget that we have inherited the dream to be great and successful also. Because we belong to Christ, we are the true children of Abraham and God's promise to Abraham also belongs to you.

The only difference between you and Oprah is that you have yet to cultivate your gifts. Do you think for one moment that when Oprah began doing her syndicated talk show that she said to herself, "God created me to be a talk show host and that's it"? Absolutely not. We limit our levels of success and our exposure to new and beneficial opportunities because of the inherited tunnel vision invested in us by our parents, grandparents, and childhood experiences. The formula of the olden days, was to work hard at the same job for 40 years and then retire with your fingers crossed praying to God almighty that you can survive on your pension until you die. God has an impeccable record and I find it hard to believe that while creating you, He stopped at you being a one hit wonder. We are born with this greatness gene that gives us the authority to do and be whatever we want only IF you are willing to work and nurture those gifts to your advantage.

I never knew that I was an inspirational or motivational speaker until I was asked to speak at a banquet for a local organization for a group of women. I can remember driving to the venue and thinking to myself, "Lord what am I going to say to this room full of women?" I remember pulling an envelope out of my purse and I began to jot down things that came to my mind about nurturing our young women and related it to the task of nurturing a garden. To my surprise, I guess I really was an inspirational speaker! I stress "to my surprise" because nothing is a surprise to God and nothing catches Him by surprise. It's moments like this that I have to step back and realize that this was the manifestation of yet another gift and accepted that challenge with grace!

Had I declined the invitation to speak, I would have missed out on identifying one of the best gifts that I have. I was later contacted the following year to speak for this same organization. Not only was I excited about the opportunity, but even more ecstatic when attendees from the previous year came up to me to say they remembered me and asked if I were speaking again. You simply cannot lose. **You have the greatness gene!**

> **You were designed**
>
> **to be GREAT and there is nothing**
>
> **you can do about it.**

Now, About Those Gifts of Yours....Let's revisit!

1. _____

2. _____

3. _____

4. _____

5. _____

Sometimes, it seems that getting buy in on your vision is so difficult. Almost depressing. This is when you realize that it's not your vision. It's the environment. Be willing to move! Physically and mentally.

#showupempty

Uncomfortable Enough To Move

While writing this book, I checked into a hotel about 45 minutes away from home. I wanted to relax, but I also wanted to write to the tone of a different scenery. Something I hadn't seen, people I didn't know, and a new environment. I planned to be gone for three nights. Once I arrived at the hotel I thought, this is "OK" for what I'm here for. As the night went on, I began to be a bit uncomfortable; as if I were settling but I decided to stick it out. The next day, something else happened that made me realize that this simply was not where I was supposed to be. So, I packed up within 15 minutes and was headed to a new hotel. Yes I know, it sounds a bit over the top, but I very quickly realized the lesson in this. I was never going to be comfortable there because it was never meant for me to be comfortable in that place.

Sometimes, you too may feel as though were you are a bit comfortable and you must know that this is normal. This is what you can expect when you are not fully maximizing your potential and using your gifts.

Expect to be uncomfortable. Expect to be unhappy and unfulfilled. Hopefully, you will begin to notice that these feelings exist simply because you were never meant to stay in this place. You've got to get up and move!

That feeling should serve as a reminder that you have not yet tapped into those gifts designed and created just for you. There is a blessing in your discomfort!

Gift Check!

Can you identify a time that you were forced into doing something that felt uncomfortable?

_____

_____

_____

During that uncomfortable time, was there a part of you that found joy? (No matter how small)

_____

_____

_____

Jot down a few POSITIVE things that you remember about this time. What lessons are learned from this?

_____

_____

_____

Show Up Empty

> Showing Up Empty does not just require that you use all of your gifts and talents, It also requires that you rid your heart of hatred, grudges, and bitterness.
>
> #showupempty

Trash Day

This was the hardest chapter for me to write. Why? Because writing this chapter meant that I had to practice what I was preaching. I was guilty of holding on to grudges against people in both my personal and professional life whom I felt had let me down. People that I expected more from, where not doing or saying what I felt I needed, and I was mortified!! What I came to realize was that I can't make anyone treat me the way that I felt that I needed to be treated. I also realized that the longer I held on to bitterness, anger, and grudges, the further away I was from Showing Up Empty. Let me be the first to say that this was by no means an easy task, and it took lots of prayer and talking to God to get me through this. **I had to understand and know that God is not the author of confusion and while He was trying to work in me, He couldn't work around my mess that I chose to hoard! (This will be hard to highlight so just look at it REAL hard! :-)**

To get to your NEXT level, you too have got to rid yourself of any malice that resides in your heart. **(I KNOW this is hard but do it anyway)** Not only are you wasting time and energy, but you are also delaying blessings in your life. Detach take out the trash, and get into p

This page intentionally left blank. We will just call this the "Trash Page" :-)

Use this page to identify those things in your life that needs to go.

Bread Crumbs

I always knew that my career would be in health care. There was never any doubt about this in my mind. I was so fascinated and amused with everything that had anything to do with health care and caring for people. I began my journey as a telephone operator in a large health care system. I remember my station being in the rear of the building near the employee entrance. I would sit there and watch the doctors, nurses, and drug representatives enter all day long all while thinking to myself, "I can't wait to be like them!" It wasn't long before I was inquiring about other positions within the organization. I had to get out of that back station, so I could see what else was going on in the building. From my view, I could feel the hustle and bustle of things happening, but I couldn't see or feel it for myself.

Shortly thereafter, I transferred to the front desk and began working as a Registration Clerk and a Coder. I was so excited to be right in the middle of it all.

It wasn't long before I had mastered this position and began to get itsy all over again. From my new station, I could see the pharmacy buzzing with activity and patients all day long. Yes you guessed it, I got the itch again. The itch to learn something new AGAIN! I inquired and before I knew it, I was a Licensed Pharmacy Technician and filling prescriptions like a champ.

Throughout my life, I have always been blessed to learn things very quickly, and could absorb information with the ability to apply it without difficulty. I can remember being excited about my changing positions and learning new job duties and sharing it with my dad. My feelings were truly hurt when I heard his response. It wasn't what I expected or wanted to hear. He said to me, "I've been on the same job over 35 years.

You need to get a job and stay there." That statement is what I know was the statement that would ignite the entrepreneurial fire in me. I can remember wondering why I had to pick just one thing and do that for the rest of my life.

Why can't I keep learning new things? Clearly, I was good in these areas and mastering new task was something that came very easy for me.

What my dad saw as job hopping, I saw as leaving breadcrumbs. That I could later use as my foundation for my success. Every position that I transitioned into as a health care professional, was essential in my success a nurse and also in my success as an Entrepreneur. When I realized that I wanted and needed to be my own boss with my own rules, I also realized that I had dropped bread crumbs that I was now able to pick up and build future and my legacy with. I learned after many disappointments in college and jobs that I simply did not like or felt was not challenging, that it is quite alright to build your own bridge to success and then walk it with p

I had to convince myself daily that the road I chose to travel didn't have to look like the curriculum and syllabus that sat before me on numerous occasions. I can't tell you how many times I have sat in interviews with executives who scratched their heads as they scanned my resume. I would often hear, "I've never seen such an array of education and experience!" Hearing that made me smile on the inside knowing that the decisions I made and chances that I took were finally being seen as EXTRAORDINARY and achieved that by vowing to **SHOW UP EMPTY!**

It may not always make sense or look "right" on this journey but you have to remain confident in your faith and know that you were designed and built for this! (Highlight this!)

I did not come from a long line of entrepreneurs or business owners, imagine how I felt trying to explaining to my family of blue collar workers that I was starting a business. This was unheard of. My ancestors are hard working people from the South and I was quickly becoming the odd representative.

It was the "norm" that you work hard, keep your head down, be grateful and repeat. However, I wanted to work hard, make my own rules, try new things, create, build, apply, teach, share, and invent. Showing Up Empty requires the ability to stand alone and to be able to go against the grain. You will never be empty if you follow in the footsteps of others and not walk in the purpose tailor made for you.

Your gifts were not intended to fit you, her, him, and them so stop trying to make people be a part of what you're doing. Sometimes it will feel as though you are standing alone because you were created to be great, and you can't be great and normal. Your gifts were created and molded to fit you so stand out and do it! (Go back and read the last three sentences again. That's for you!)

Gift Check

Can you identify with the Breadcrumb Analogy? _____

What breadcrumbs have you dropped along your journey?

_____
_____
_____
_____
_____
_____

How do you plan to apply these breadcrumbs to your life/career?

_____
_____
_____
_____
_____
_____

Assembly Required

Assembling things that I've purchased have always been liberating to me. It makes me feel as if I achieved something grand all by myself or conquered a very big giant. I always poor all of the contents out of the box and began to work diligently but without reading the instructions. More times than not, I would find myself having to disassemble the project only to read the instructions and then assemble the right way.

I was well into my thirties before I realized that the instructions for that bookshelf were very similar to the instructions for my life. The bible was created to be the best set of instructions that you and I will ever need. Literally, everything you face on this journey has instructions for you to read and comprehend before facing any challenges and will also help you while you're going through them. Not only are there instructions, but there are also "cliff notes" which I refer to as promises of God that backs up the instructions and reinforces their value.

To Show Up Empty requires work and lots of it. Some of which will drain you at times and make you doubt that the path you've chosen is indeed where you should be. The good thing about this process is that you are attempting to use every gift in spite of its outcome. This alone is activation of unimaginable faith! It also shows that you can now trust God to know the even if this gift isn't the "big" one, there is something in this process that you must learn on your way to identifying the next gift. Can I give you this valuable piece of information? When you are emptying out the right way, God will make sure that your cup is never empty! **(Definitely Worth Highlighting!)**

The important thing to remember here is that all of the gifts uniquely designed for you are packaged with instructions which are accessible to you. All you need to do is open and activate the word and promises of God to help you along this journey.

I thought you might like to know a few of the promises God has made to us. Turn the page!

The Promises

2 Timothy 3:16 All scripture is given by inspiration of God, and is profitable for doctrine, for reproof, for correction, for instruction in righteousness.

2 Peter 1:4 Through these He has given us his very great and precious promises, so that through them you may participate in the divine nature and escape the corruption in the world caused by evil doers.

Jeremiah 29:11 "For I know the plans I have for you," declares the Lord, "plans to prosper you and not to harm you, plans to give you hope and a future.

Matthew 11:28 "Come to me, all you who are weary and burdened, and I will give you rest."

Philippians 4:19 And my God will meet all your needs according to His glorious riches in Jesus Christ.

Parallel Bible New International Version

You Be The Expert

What is an expert anyway? Who determines the guidelines for being an expert? Why can't you be an expert? After all, you experienced it right? You went through it right? You came out of it with a story to tell right? Then who better than you to tell that story? **Who or what in your life have you allowed to dictate what you are good at? (This is good stuff!)**

An expert is defined as "having or showing special skill or knowledge because of what you have been taught or what you have experienced. (Merriam Webster)

That's you! Every opportunity for you to learn something new, use a gift or talent that you have not used before, or to enhance a skill that you already possess increases your opportunity to **Show Up Empty!** It may be frightening at first, but you've got to remember and stand on the fact that this is what you were made for.

This is what is intended. **God wants you to use every gift He has delicately placed inside of you. It makes Him happy when we stretch past fear and doubt and push for greater. (Worth Highlighting)** Showing Up Empty won't be easy, and it was designed that way. You will pushed into areas that are unfamiliar to you and areas that may seem uncomfortable. It's in these times that God expects you to "tag Him in" as your partner. Remember, this didn't catch Him by surprise. This is only new for you. You're greatness is intentional. **(Highlight This!)**

> **Each and every trial, challenge, and struggle in your life was strategically placed there for your gain.**
>
> **Build from these experiences.**

Proverbs 4:7 "In all of thy getting, get an understanding"

Show Up Empty

Invest In You

The best investment that you can make is in you. You should always seek ways to learn more, to earn more, to increase your knowledge and your wealth. Reaching new heights and achieving new milestones is a wonderful feeling that should be celebrated, but you can't stay there. There are so many opportunities and avenues that offers seminars, seminars, workshops and conferences about the things that interest you. It's also a good idea to reach outside the box and attend a few that you have no interest in because it's usually in those that new ideas are blossomed. Exploring learning opportunities is also a great way to network with others and form long lasting and beneficial professional relationships. You must look at the big picture. You can't just say that this will not be just another conference or meeting. No, you must look at this as an opportunity that you will enjoy and learn from. Get out of the box and create your own possibilities.

Let's change your way of thinking!

- I'm traveling to another state
- I will meet new people
- I will get to explore area that I'm not familiar with
- I will try new exotic foods
- I will lean from experts in this field
- I will engage with others to enhance my own gifts and talents

How Can You Invest **MORE** In You?

1._____

2._____

3._____

4._____

5._____

> **Every opportunity is an OPPORTUNITY to learn and to grow if you can see it that way.**

Show Up Empty

"For my thoughts are not your thoughts, neither are your ways my ways," declares the LORD."

Using the Erasable Ink Pen

We can all attest to writing plans, goals, and dreams. We can also attest to things not going as we planned. You may have even settled into something that looks and feels okay but deep down inside you know that this is not IT. Something about where you've settled just does not feel right.

I can honestly say that I'm actually grateful that God didn't allow some of my dreams to manifest as I thought they should have. That's one of the benefits of serving a Sovereign God. He does what He wants, when\He wants to and our permission is never a factor. **One of the greatest things you can learn in leadership is how to fold! To continue doing something that is not producing GOOD FRUIT, is pointless. It does not mean that you have failed, this just may be a sign to let you know that what was meant to be learned from this, has been learned.**

You have reached a plateau. Debrief and move on! You've got more work to do. (You know what to do here!)

It is both important and comforting to know that you can always trust God's plans for your life. This may require some erasing, deleting, or rerouting on your part, but it will be well worth it in the end. **None of this is to say that you should stop dreaming and setting goals, it just simply means that you have to alert enough to acknowledge when God is trying** to reroute you for greater. (Where's Your Highlighter?)

Proverbs 18:16 "A man's gift makes room for him and brings him before great men."

Show Up Empty

Hustling Vs. Gifting

The difference between the two is often misconstrued. When one is hustling, he or she will find themselves constantly having to pitch something to someone, or to convince others to believe in their mission to gain buy in. When you begin to activate your gifts, they really will make room for you **(Proverbs 18:16)** The pitch is in the gift itself! When you are developing the gifts God has given you, it's not necessary to work as hard to advertise your gifts. There will be no need for you to run a capital campaign to get others to support what you're doing. In God's time, you will have everything and everyone that you need. You will begin to receive calls and invites from people that you never even knew existed. All you will need to do is **Show Up** and be prepared.

The other great part of the verse referenced here is that the gift will also take you places that your hustle never could.

When gifts are activated, it's like being upgraded to first class on your flight. The atmosphere changes, the people around you are equally gifted and all while you are in first class, the blessings just keep on coming. Not only will you be elevated to the new heights of where your blessings and favor are stored, but while you are there people will go out of their way to make sure you're comfortable and that you have everything that you need.

If only we could trust God enough to lose the fear of not knowing exactly what those blessings are and what they consist of, we could began to experience this greatness much sooner.

Exercise:

Place your left and then right hand over your left chest. Can you feel that? That's your purpose and your passion!

Get acquainted with this feeling.

> It is perfectly alright to ask God for help when identifying your gifts. Your faith activates blessings and He loves when we seek Him.
>
> #showupempty

Show Up Empty

Palpitations & Purpose

I find it exciting to talk with people who have not yet identified their gifts. They are in that place that I like to refer to as the "waiting room". It is in this place that they are trying to find their purpose, what they should be doing, and how will they know when they have found their purpose.

I say this is exciting because I get to explain this process to them in a way that takes me back to my nursing days. I relate the finding your purpose to palpitations because of the severity of the two. A person experiencing palpitations will tell you that when it happens, it startles them. It catches them off guard and initially they cannot tell exactly what is going on with their body. If the feeling has never been experienced, a certain level of anxiety and fear may develop. The palpitation itself is usually not so serious but it's alerting the body that something more pressing is really the need for concern.

When you have been in contact with your gift, you will know because of the palpitations. When talking about your gift and purpose causing slight fluttering in your chest, you know that you have arrived. When just mere conversation about what is rooted in you and so very important to you causes you to become excited, then you know it's your purpose!

When you can no longer settle for other things taking up time and pace in your life, then you know once again that this is your purpose. It has a heartbeat and one that is very strong. That beat is a reminder to you that it's alive and just waiting for you to activate it and began to see it manifest in your life.

Gift Check!

What "palpitation" have you felt? What do you perceive to be you purpose?

_____

_____

_____

_____

_____

_____

_____

_____

John 10:27 My sheep listen to my voice; I know them, and they follow me.

Seek God For Clarity-He's The Master Builder

Imagine buying a new home. In most cases it's already built and you have little say in its actual design or construction. You simply move in and add your personal touch to make this place comfortable and home. How awesome is it that you have a personal relationship with the master builder, the one who created your destiny and who already knows your ending? With this relationship, YOU CAN NOT FAIL!

Nothing pleases God more than for us to seek Him at all times for clarity and direction. He wants us to come to Him when we are unsure of what moves to make and what routes to take to get there. Even when we have gotten off track and made a few mistakes, He still wants to hear from us. We spend valuable time trying to figure out what to do when all we need to do is go back to Master Builder who is responsible for blue prints. He has all of the answers!

So, take EVERYTHING to God in prayer. All of your ideas, your questions, your dreams, and your visions and watch Him work.

Master The Art of Service

#showupempty

Show Up Empty

Are You Serving? If not, let's get you started! I will even give you th first one.

1. <u>Community</u>
2. _____
3. _____
4. _____
5. _____

Fail Until You Fly

Like most good things in life, Showing Up Empty comes with a price. [It]'s not usual to become comfortable and complacent in daily routines and [c]hoices because it's easier than stepping out into the unknown. This journey [is] intended to make you comfortable so that daily you are reminded that you [a]re not yet empty.

In 2012, I was so excited to finally complete my Master's degree in [H]ealth Care Administration. I was a young mother at the age of 17, and [w]orked my behind off to finally get to this stage in my life. In my last [se]mester, I was on target with my classes and only needed an elective to [gr]aduate. I figured that this last semester I would just cruise on auto pilot. [A]fter all, I had mastered all of my other classes so this would be a walk in [th]e park. I elected to take an online Human Resources course because [ev]eryone can use HR right?

The instructor was the most detached and unconcerned educator that I [ha]d ever encountered. It wasn't long before I could see that this class was [go]ing to hell in a hand basket. You see, we were required to work in groups [wh]ile each of the students in this class were spread out across the 50 states. [Af]ter numerous attempts of trying to communicate my concerns about the challenges and lack of communication, my concerns went without actions. Because we were considered to be a "group", the lack of work by others in the online class also reflected on me as an individual. I had worked so very hard to get to this point. Nearly 17 years after graduating high school, I was finally about to adorn my gown and walk away as a graduate student. Imagine my disappointment when I was notified that the grade of "C" that I received was not acceptable as a graduate student. I was crushed, I worked so hard and come so far, this could not be happening. I fought, I wrote letters, I appealed, I forwarded emails as proof that I cried out!

After several months of waiting for the decision from the powers that be, I was informed that the board would not over turn their decision. Throughout the two years it took to pursue this degree, I worked full-time as a nurse, I had a daughter in high school, I prepared to open my own business and this was to be the icing on the cake for me. Everything inside of me said to quit! This was too much. Clearly, I was not cut out for this and maybe Master's degree was not in the plans for me. I cried, I was angry, and I was so disappointed. After a month, I reapplied to a different university for the same program. I had accepted the fact that I would be repeating this entire program, but **I did not accept defeat! (Highlight This)**

Failure is whatever you accept and allow it to be. How are you going to plant your failure? As failure or as fertilizer? We all know the potential of fertilizer and its purpose. Choose Ye Wisely! :-)

I chose to not look at this situation as a failure, but as an extraordinary learning opportunity exclusively designed by God just for me. My faith needed more exercise! He wanted to show me AGAIN, just how great He was and how much tenacity he had given me.

"I have seen something else under the sun. The race is not to the swift or the battle to the strong, nor does food come to the wise or wealth to the brilliant or favor to the learned; but time and chance happen to the all.

Ecclesiastics 9:11 NIV

Failures Or Fertilizer?

Take a moment and reflect on some of those things that you have written off as failures. Were they really failures or fertilizer for your **NEXT?**

_____

_____

_____

_____

> Not every gift and talent will jump out at you.
>
> The most subtle confirmations are usually the most powerful ones
>
> #showupempty

What if the very failure or mistake that you are trying so hard to hide is the very thing that God allowed to happen just so you could be a blessing to someone else?

#showupempty

Show Up Empty

Let Them See You Scars

Fear and failing oftentimes will make us shy away from being transparent. It's just instinctive for us as humans to not want others to see what we have done wrong. Without realizing it, the very things that we are trying so desperately to hide, are the same things that God wants us to allow others to see. Others look and your success and not your journey, so they see where you are but not how you arrived. **The mistakes you've made can be just the encouragement that someone else needs! (Good stuff!)** The journey is bound to present several challenges, and it's up to you to decide just what you want to do with them. Will continue to hide them, or will you place them on the mantle for others to see and learn from? While you are making your decisions, keep in mind that God favors your obedience and sometimes your blessings are just on the other side of this!

Serve As If Your Life Depends On It!

One of the most important roles that we all should work to perfect is that of service. The number of gifts you have nor their ability to produce financial gain should ever supersede good ole fashion service to others. Whether it's in the community, in the church, or in the schools, service is definitely required to consider yourself "empty".

Remember how we talked about the bible being our guide for Showing Up Empty? It commands us to serve and love one another regardless of status or color. Not only is it commanded of us, but is also a very rewarding experience to serve and help others. There are great benefits that can only be received when you serve. The experience teaches patience, keeps you humble, and builds character. All of which you will need on your journey to Showing Up Empty! Although be it sad, there are so many who have yet to identify how and who to serve. There is no special formula to serve, just identify where the need is and start there.

What will be your area of service? Will you mentor? Will you read to the elderly? Will you tutor children? Whatever you decide, do it to the best of your ability and always remember that there's someone out there who needs just what you have been equipped with. Give freely of yourself and watch the promises of God come full circle in your life.

How Will I Know I'm Empty?

Here is the most honest answer I have for this question: **You Won't!** This journey was never designed to allow you to "check your balance". You can't log in and see if you are empty! We were created to give, serve, love, and bear the burdens of our brothers and sisters without a maximum capacity.

Continue to seek out your gifts (plural) and your purpose. You have so much to give to so many. **"IN THE SAME WAY, LET YOUR LIGHT SHINE BEFORE OTHERS, THAT THEY MAY SEE YOUR GOOD AND GLORIGY YOUR FATHER IN HEAVEN." (Matthew 5:16)**

Keep working until the day is done. When you see HIS face, then you will know that you are EMPTY!

I Dare You To Show Up Empty!

You Cannot lose.

#Showupempty

Notes

Show Up Empty

Notes

Notes

Show Up Empty

Notes

Notes

Show Up Empty

About The Author

Tawanda Story is the fifth of six children born to Wayne and Velma Story. She was born in St. Louis, Missouri and raised in Alorton, Illinois, a small city just outside of East St. Louis, Illinois. Tawanda is a proud product of the East St. Louis School District 189. She is a Licensed Practical Nurse who also holds Bachelor's Degree from Webster University (St. Louis, Missouri) in Business Administration and a Master's Degree from Lindenwood University in Healthcare Administration. (Belleville, Illinois)

Tawanda is the Founder and Executive Director of No Senior Left Behind, nonprofit organization whose mission and purpose is to make sure seniors and their families have all that they need as well as access to resources. She resides in O'Fallon, Illinois were she fulfills her best title as daughter and caregiver to the BEST father in the world! She is the mother of one beautiful and talented daughter Paris Olivia.

Tawanda is forever grateful and humble to God for the calling on her life to help and serve others but more so for the commandment to

Show Up Empty!

Let's Keep The Movement Going!

Show Up Empty!!!

Twitter

@Showupempty

Facebook

Show Up Empty

Tawanda Story

Instagram

Show Up Empty

For book signings and speaking engagements, please email

Showupempty@gmail.com

Made in the USA
Charleston, SC
09 April 2016